THE AUDUBON SOCIETY POCKET GUIDES

A Chanticleer Press Edition

Richard Spellenberg
Professor of Biology
New Mexico State University

Ann H. Whitman
Editor

Western Region

FAMILIAR FLOWERS OF NORTH AMERICA

Alfred A. Knopf, New York

This is a Borzoi Book
Published by Alfred A. Knopf, Inc.

All rights reserved. Copyright 1986 under the
International Union for the protection of literary and
artistic works (Berne). Published in the United States by
Alfred A. Knopf, Inc., New York, and simultaneously in
Canada by Random House of Canada Limited, Toronto.
Distributed by Random House, Inc., New York.

Prepared and produced by Chanticleer Press, Inc.,
New York.
Color reproductions by Nievergelt Repro AG,
Zurich, Switzerland.
Typeset by Dix Type Inc., Syracuse, New York.
Printed and bound by Dai Nippon, Tokyo, Japan.

Published October 1986
Reprinted once
Third Printing, August 1990

Library of Congress Catalog Number: 86-045586
ISBN: 0-394-74844-1

Trademark "Audubon Society" used by publisher under
license from the National Audubon Society, Inc.

Contents

How to Use This Guide

Wherever there is soil that has not been covered by pavement, plants manage to establish themselves and produce flowers. Even in cities, wildflowers are a pleasure to find and identify.

Coverage

This new guide covers 80 of the most common native wildflowers of the West—species that anyone is likely to encounter. Our geographical range is bounded by the Pacific Ocean on the west, and on the east by the 100th meridian, extending from Edwards Plateau in Texas northward through Oklahoma and westward through eastern Colorado, Wyoming, and Montana, and Canada, along the eastern foothills of the Rocky Mountains. A companion volume covers flowers east of the Rockies.

Organization

This easy-to-use guide is divided into three parts: introductory essays, illustrated accounts of the flowers, and appendices.

Introduction

As a basic introduction, the essay "Identifying Flowers" suggests some guidelines for discovering the identity of an unfamiliar wildflower. "The Form of a Flower" describes the basic structure of various families of flowers. Black-and-white drawings illustrate different kinds of flowers, leaves, and clusters.

The Flowers	This section contains 80 color plates arranged visually, according to the color and shape of the bloom. Facing each illustration is a description of the most important characteristics of the flower, including range and habitat. The introductory paragraph describes look-alikes and relatives, among other topics. A black-and-white drawing of each plant supplements the photograph.
Appendices	Featured here is "Families and Their Members," an alphabetical listing of all the flower families in the guide, with the names and page numbers of the species represented.
A Word of Caution	Many wildflowers are edible, and some have been used for centuries as medicines, aphrodisiacs, or food. The interesting histories of these plants have been included here, but this book is not a guide to edible plants. There are many toxic species in North America, and some can be fatal; to the inexperienced eye, these poisonous plants may be difficult to tell from innocuous look-alikes. Do not risk making a mistake; do not eat any plant you find growing in the wild.

Identifying Flowers

You will easily learn to identify many wildflowers by paying attention to three general kinds of features: where the plant grows, its vegetative characteristics, and the characteristics of the flower. Once you learn what questions to ask yourself, you will gain a general understanding of all the plants on the continent.

Location

Where is the plant found? Botanical exploration of North America is reasonably complete, and there are few surprises left. If you think you have identified a plant, but the range description does not match, the identification is probably not correct, although the plant may be a close relative of the wildflower described. Some species have very exacting habitat requirements.

Stems and Leaves

What are the characteristics of the stems and leaves? Features of the stem contribute to the general aspect, or habit, of the plant. Does the stem branch? If so, does the branching occur only at the top or the bottom? Is the plant tall? Short? Short and matted? Are all the leaves and flowers attached at one point near the ground (rosettes)?

Are the leaves divided (compound) or not (simple)? If simple, what is their shape? Are the edges plain, lobed,

8

or toothed? If the leaves are compound, are they palmate (shaped like a hand)? Pinnate (like a feather)? More than once pinnately compound? How are they placed on the stem? Is there only one at a point on the stem (alternate)? Two at a point (opposite or paired)? More than two (in rings or "whorled")?

Flowers
For the beginner, the symmetry of the flower and nature of the petals are the most important aspects to study. Is the blossom actually composed of many small flowers surrounded by a ring of green bracts? (If so, the plant is probably a member of the daisy family.) As you look at the flower, is it radially symmetrical, like a wheel? Or is it bilaterally symmetrical—that is, can it be divided only down the center into two equal halves?

How many petals are there? Are they joined or separate? If joined, do they form a tube, trumpet, funnel, bowl, or saucer? Are petal lobes evident?

The position of the ovary—the part of the flower that produces the fruit—can be important in identification. Is the ovary in the center of the flower, with all the other parts attached at its base? Or is the ovary inferior, with the parts all attached at the top, making the ovary visible from the side of the flower?

The Form of a Flower

The way a flower looks has a significance beyond natural beauty: Form and color are important in successful reproduction. A flower's development must be precisely coordinated and timed to mesh with the activities and abilities of its animal pollinators. For these reasons, the form of a flower tends to be complex, precise, and stable. The flower parts—the stamens, sepals, petals, and ovaries—must function together precisely, while the color and odor attract pollinators. The nectaries—and often the pollen as well—provide incentives for insects or birds to visit the flowers.

Generally speaking, very similar flowers are members of closely related groups—species, genera, and families. A knowledge of family characteristics provides a general familiarity with wildflowers throughout temperate North America. Learning a few very large families, such as the buttercup, pea, or sunflower (daisy) family, gives the satisfaction of recognizing something familiar and eases the burden of trying to distinguish among a thousand or more species.

Evolution Plants have evolved at different rates. In general, more advanced species or families have fewer individual parts (stamens, ovaries, petals, and sepals), and those parts are joined to some degree. Fairly primitive families, such as the buttercup family, have separate sepals, separate petals, many stamens, and many separate ovaries. Members of the more advanced rose family have similar flowers, but the bases of the petals, the sepals, and the stamens are all joined to form a cup, or hypanthium, around the ovary or ovaries.

One of the most advanced families is the sunflower family. This huge group may give the beginner some trouble, because what appears to be a flower is actually a head made up of hundreds of tiny flowers; the "petals" surrounding the head are called rays. Each of the tiny flowers that make up the head has an inferior ovary that produces a single seed.

Fusion   Sometimes, similar flower parts are fused; this adaptation encourages pollination by visiting insects or birds. Members of the morning glory, waterleaf, and borage families, for example, all have five petals that are fused; in the morning glories, the petals form a funnel, while in the other two groups, the flower clusters form "fiddle-necks."

The Number of Parts   Many wildflowers have just a few of each kind of flower part. The mustard family, for example, is easy to

11

recognize by its four sepals, four petals, six stamens (four long ones and two short ones), and an ovary that is divided into two chambers by a papery partition. Members of the evening primrose family also have four sepals and four petals, but they differ in having either four or eight stamens; the ovary is inferior. Lilies have three sepals (which look like petals in some species), three petals, six stamens, and an ovary with three chambers. Members of the iris family have three stamens and bear the ovary beneath all the other parts of the flower. Like many families, the mallows have five petals and five sepals; the stamens are joined at the base in the middle of the flower, and look like a small shaving brush.

Symmetry   Many flowers have radial symmetry, like a wheel: You can draw an imaginary line through the center, and the same structure will be evident on each side of the line. Other flowers have responded to animal pollinators by developing bilateral symmetry—a left and a right side. The pea family is a large group of bilaterally symmetrical flowers. Members of the family are easy to recognize; they have a large upper petal, two smaller side petals, and two lower petals that are joined like the keel of a

12

boat. There are ten stamens; nine are usually joined, and the uppermost one is then independent.

Some flowers with fused petals are also bilaterally symmetrical. The members of the mint family are easy to recognize; they have a four-sided stem, opposite leaves, and (usually) a minty odor; the distinctive flowers have two or four stamens, and the ovary divides into four hard segments, or nutlets. Most of the showy members of the snapdragon family have four pollen-bearing stamens (others have two or five); the ovary forms a capsule with two chambers.

The orchids are highly advanced flowers with three petal-like sepals and three petals; the lower one of the three is always different from the two upper ones. The central complex of one or two stamens is joined to the style (the narrow part of the female portion of the flower above the ovary); the ovary itself is inferior.

There are thousands of wildflowers in North America, and no single book can include them all. By learning to recognize family characteristics, however, it is possible to gain a solid basis that will serve you well as you become more expert at flower identification.

Parts of a Flower

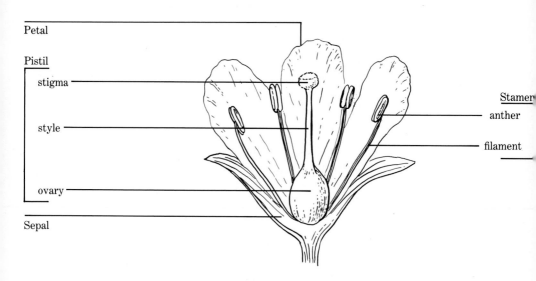

Petal

Pistil
  stigma

  style

  ovary

Sepal

Stamen
anther

filament

Disk Flower   Ray Flower

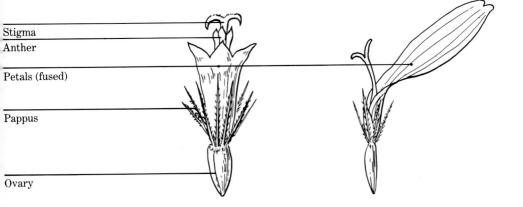

Stigma

Anther

Petals (fused)

Pappus

Ovary

Composite Flower

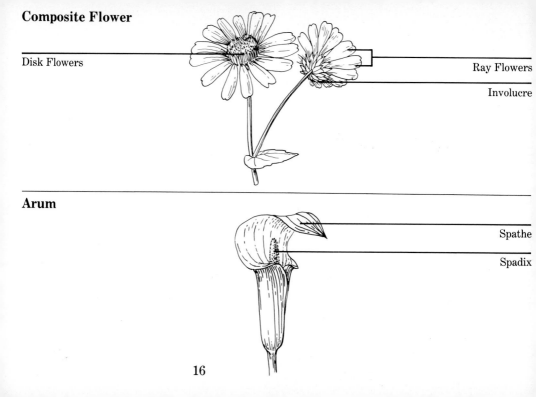

Disk Flowers

Ray Flowers

Involucre

Arum

Spathe

Spadix

16

Iris

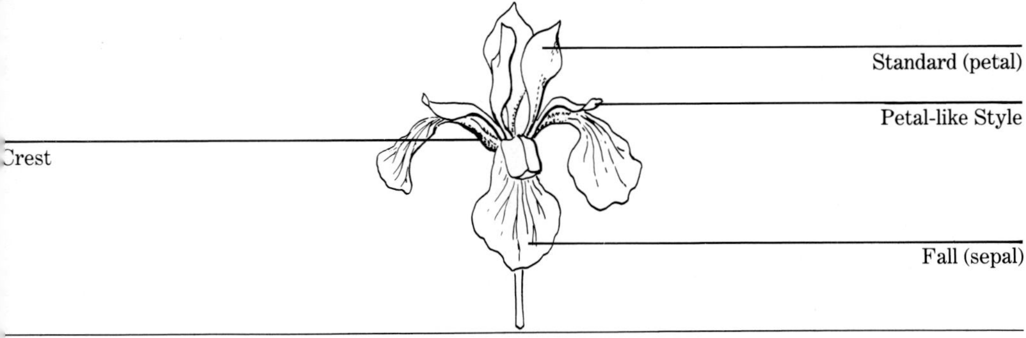

Standard (petal)

Petal-like Style

Crest

Fall (sepal)

Pea Flower

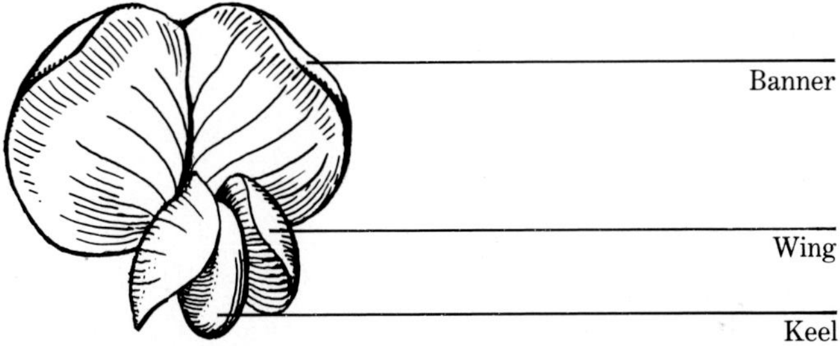

Banner

Wing

Keel

17

Cluster Types

Raceme	Spike

Corymb

Umbel

Cyme

Leaf Types

Lance-shaped

Oval

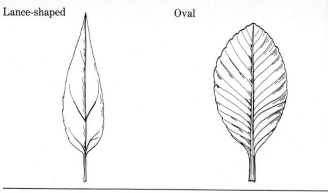

Pinnate

Opposite

Toothed

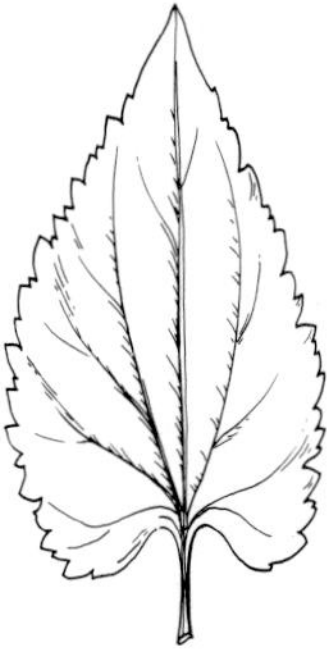

Lobed

Palmate

Alternate

Clasping

Basal

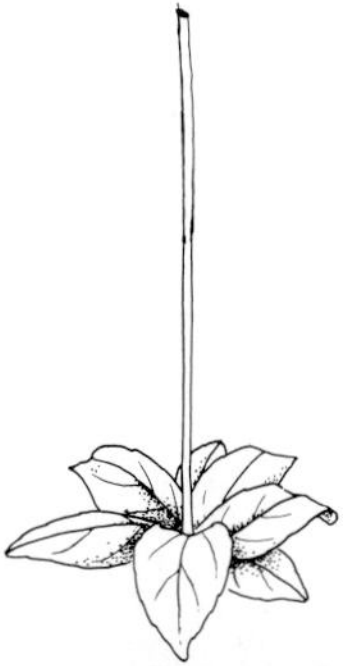

THE FLOWERS

Sulphur Flower *Eriogonum umbellatum*

Sulphur Flower belongs to a huge, diverse western North American genus, wild buckwheat. Its members have tiny white, yellow, pink, or reddish flowers with six petal-like parts; the flowers are held in five-toothed cups (involucres); and the ovary forms a tiny, three-sided fruit, which is seedlike. This makes the genus easy to identify, but species identification is difficult. Sulphur Flower blooms from June to August.

Identification   Long, erect stalks with tiny yellow or cream flowers in balls at the ends of branches; leaves at the base. Height: 4–12″. Flower clusters 2–4″ wide, the branches all attaching to 1 point at top of stalk. Flowers about ¼″ long; hairy on the outside. At base of flower cluster is a circle of small, leaflike bracts. Leaves ½–1½″ long, on slender stalks; generally oval, about 2–3 times longer than wide; very hairy below; clustered at the ends of short, woody branches.

Habitat   Dry sagebrush deserts and foothills to alpine ridges.

Range   British Columbia to S. California, east to the eastern flank of the Rocky Mts. from Colorado to Montana.

Stream Violet *Viola glabella*

To one acquainted solely with the purple, sweet-scented florist's violet (*V. odorata*), it may be surprising that many of the western species have yellow or white flowers, and that the cheery-faced Pansy (*V. tricolor*), from Europe, is in the same genus. Many wild violets produce showy flowers early in the season and inconspicuous flowers near the base later. This wildflower is also called Pioneer Violet or Smooth Yellow Violet. It blooms from March to July.

Identification Cheery, bilateral yellow flowers face outward, hanging from the curved top of a stalk; stems leaning, with leaves only on the upper third. Height: 2–12″. Flowers ½–¾″ wide; lower petal has maroon lines at base and a pouch protruding backward under flower; 2 lateral, bearded petals with maroon lines; 2 upper petals, yellow on back. Leaves heart-shaped, 1¼–3½″ long; finely toothed on edges; on long stalks.

Habitat In moist woods or along streams.

Range Alaska to the southern Sierra Nevada of California, east to W. Montana.

Plains Wallflower *Erysimum asperum*

The four yellow petals suggest that this showy wildflower belongs to the mustard family; the two short and four long stamens confirm it. Westward, this flower intergrades with the Western Wallflower (*E. capitatum*), which has erect pods nearly pressed against the stem. The Western Wallflower may be yellow through orange to almost rust, depending on its location. In the West, species were used medicinally in several ways—to alleviate chest pains, to cure pneumonia, and to prevent sunburn. Plains Wallflower, often forming dense stands of bright yellow along roads, blooms from April to July.

Identification Dense clusters of bright yellow flowers atop leafy stems, branched in upper part. Height: 6–14″. Flowers ½–1″ wide; the 4 petals have a slender base and a broad tip spreading at right angles. Leaves lance-shaped, 1–5″ long, sometimes with teeth. Pod very slender, 4-sided; 3–5″ long; projects upward at an angle.

Habitat Open hills and plains.

Range Central Canada to Texas, mostly east of the Rockies, but occurring sporadically westward.

28

California Poppy *Eschscholtzia californica*

"Poppies, golden poppies, gleaming in the sun," begins a children's song honoring California's state flower. When blooming profusely, it will carpet hillsides with a mantle of fiery orange or deep yellow-gold that can be seen from miles away. The flowers are responsive to sunlight, opening in the strong light of morning and closing early in the evening or on cloudy days. Of the several *Eschscholtzia* species, some with much smaller flowers, this is the only one with a conspicuous pink rim at the base of the ovary or pod. It blooms in the West from February to September.

Identification   Flowers bright orange or gold-yellow and orange, cup-shaped; leaves fernlike. Height: 8–24″. Flowers are 1–2″ wide, with 4 fan-shaped petals; sepals joined into a dunce cap-shaped cone, which slides off as flower opens. Leaves bluish-green, ¾–2½″ long; repeatedly divided into very narrow segments.

Habitat   Open areas, common on road banks and grassy slopes.

Range   S. Washington to S. California, east to extreme W. Texas.

30

Subalpine Buttercup *Ranunculus eschscholtzii*

There are 30 or more buttercups in the West; the Subalpine Buttercup is among the showiest, with shiny, brilliant yellow petals that nearly hide the foliage. According to childhood lore, when the shiny petals are held close to the chin a yellow glow appears, revealing a fondness for butter. This buttercup, like other plants of the alpine, grows low to the ground, protecting it from freezing; it flowers profusely in its short growing season to attract pollinators and ensure enough seed. This species blooms as the snow melts, from June to August.

Identification Low plants with 5 shiny bright yellow petals in each flower and smooth leaves. Height: 2–10″. Flowers ¾–1½″ across, their sepals dropping as the flower opens; many stamens. Leaves ¼–1¼″ long; roundish; may have 3 shallow lobes or be divided into many narrow segments.

Habitat High mountain meadows and rocky slopes.

Range Alaska to S. California, east to the Rockies from Alberta to N. New Mexico.

Plains Pricklypear *Opuntia polyacantha*

This species introduces the complex American genus *Opuntia*, which includes the pricklypears, the less spiny Beavertail Cactus, and the treelike chollas of the Southwest. In the first two, the stems consist of flattened joints, in the last they are cylindrical. The Plains Pricklypear is mostly unloved. Low and inconspicuous, on heavily grazed rangeland it sometimes forms extensive patches, and the easily detached joints stick in the noses and throats of livestock. The Plains Pricklypear blooms from May to July.

Identification   Low mound of spiny, flat, nearly oval joints with bright yellow or sometimes magenta flowers. Height: 3–6"; clumps of stems 1–10' wide. Flowers 2–3" wide, with many petals and stamens. Stem joints bluish green, 2–4" long. Spines 2–3" long; 6–10 in each cluster; most bent down.

Habitat   Open areas on plains, in deserts, and among pinyon and juniper trees.

Range   S. British Columbia to E. Oregon and N. Arizona, east to W. Texas, Missouri, and central Canada.

34

Hooker's Evening Primrose *Oenothera hookeri*

All the evening primroses, as their name suggests, open their flowers at the end of the day. The opening is a rapid process of jerks and starts, easily observed over a short period of time. Soon after opening, the flowers are visited by hummingbird moths. Each flower closes forever the next morning. The evening primroses are diverse and common in the West, and as a group are easy to identify by their four big pale yellow or white petals and the pod that forms beneath them. Some are very low plants. This species blooms from June to September.

Identification Tall plants, usually with an unbranched stem; large flowers held well above the foliage, yellow at first but turning orange as they age the morning after opening. Height: 2–3′. Flowers have 4 broad petals 1–2″ long; stamens 8. Leaves 6–12″ long; lance-shaped, becoming progressively smaller up the stem.

Habitat Open slopes, roadsides, grassy areas, from plains well into mountains.

Range E. Washington to Baja California, east to W. Texas and S. Colorado.

36

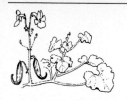

Sand Devil's Claw *Proboscidea arenaria*

This plant is in the very small unicorn-plant family, found only in the warmer parts of the Americas. As the unmistakable fruit ripens, its single "horn" divides into the two "devil's claws," which cling to the fur and legs of large animals, thereby dispersing the seeds. Both the seeds and green fruits are edible, and black fibers from the fully ripened fruit were used by Native Americans in basketry. Some related species have purple flowers, but all have the distinctive fruit. Sand Devil's Claw blooms from July to October.

Identification   Coarse plants with a heavy stem lying on the ground; bearing roundish leaves and yellow flowers, commonly flecked with brown inside. Height: about 1′; stems to 2′ long. Flowers bilateral, 1½″ long. Leaves fleshy, roundish, 1–2″ long; scalloped or shallowly lobed. Fruit a pod, about 2½″ long, with stout, upcurved horns, to 5″ long, at tip.

Habitat   Sandy or gravelly soil.

Range   Arizona, New Mexico, and Texas south to Mexico.

Yellow Fawn Lily *Erythronium grandiflorum*

These charming lilies may cover acres of ground with their cheery, nodding, clear yellow flowers. They belong to a group of about 25 in North America, all low plants with curled-back, petal-like flower segments and leaves at the stalk base; the flowers may be white, pink, or lavender. Many are called "fawn lilies," from their woodland haunts and mottled leaves, or "trout lilies," an allusion to their spotted markings. The Yellow Fawn Lily blooms from March to August, often appearing as the snow recedes.

Identification   Low plant with 1–5 nodding yellow flowers; on a stalk that grows from between 2 basal leaves. Height: 6–12″. Flowers about 2½″ across; 6 pale to bright yellow segments curled back, with tips almost touching flower stalk. Leaves 4–8″ long; only 2, at base of stalk.

Habitat   Sagebrush slopes and openings in mountain forests.

Range   S. British Columbia to N. Oregon, east to W. Colorado, Wyoming, and W. Montana.

Tiger Lily *Lilium columbianum*

This is a true lily, one of about 100 showy species in the Northern Hemisphere. Native Americans consumed the nutritious bulbs, which are often still dug up and used in gardens. Such depletion, along with logging and grazing, has reduced this lily's numbers in many places; but given a chance, it soon covers seeps and canyon sides again with its flamboyant flowers. The similar Leopard or Panther Lily (*L. pardalinum*) inhabits wet places in California; it has long anthers. The Tiger Lily blooms from May to August.

Identification   Large, showy, yellow- to red-orange flowers nodding from the top of a tall, leafy stem. Height: 2–4″. Flowers 2–3″ wide, the 6 petal-like segments curved back and speckled with deep red or purple on their inner surface; anthers ¼″ long. Leaves 2–4″ long; lance-shaped; often in rings along the stem.

Habitat   Prairies, thickets, and open forests.

Range   S. British Columbia to NW. California, east to N. Nevada and N. Idaho.

Mission Bells *Fritillaria lanceolata*

These curious lilies, with their dainty, bell-like flowers, occur where early Spanish priests founded their missions; hence the common name. There are several similar species: Spotted Mountain Bells (*F. atropurpurea*) has flowers less than ¾″ long and leaves at least 15 times longer than wide. Black Lily (*F. camchatensis*), from northwestern Washington northward, has dark purplish-brown flowers. Chocolate Lily (*F. biflora*), with unmottled, dark brown flowers, has all its leaves on the lower part of the stem. Mission Bells blooms from February to June.

Identification   Stem erect, leafy in upper part, leafless below; flowers mottled with greenish and purplish, hanging, bell-like. Height: 1–4′. Flowers bell-like, with 6 segments ¾–1½″ long. Leaves all in the upper part of the plant; lance-shaped; 1½–6″ long; usually less than 10 times longer than wide.

Habitat   Grassy or brushy flats and slopes; also in open woods.

Range   S. British Columbia to S. California, east to N. Idaho.

44

Mexican Hat *Ratibida columnaris*

The heads of this jaunty little member of the sunflower family resemble the traditional broad-brimmed, high-crowned hats worn during Mexican fiestas. They may bloom by the thousands, each little "hat" held up above the grass on a long, slender, nearly leafless stalk. Form more than color helps with identification here, for the rays may be yellow, rusty-maroon, or both. The similar Prairie Coneflower (*R. tagetes*) has a more spherical center. Mexican Hat blooms from July to October.

Identification 3–7 broad, drooping rays, yellow, brown, or yellow-brown around a long, conical, red-brown disk. Height: 1–4'. Flower heads 1–3" long, with rays ½–¾" long; stalks tough, slender, almost leafless. Central disk ½–2½" high; dark brown, composed of many tiny flowers that bloom from bottom to top. Leaves mostly at base; 1–6 " long; pinnately cleft into a few narrow segments.

Habitat Open limestone soil; common in grassy slopes, along roadsides, and on prairies.

Range From Great Plains and eastern base of Rockies west to Arizona and south to Mexico.

46

Common Sunflower *Helianthus annuus*

This plant has been cultivated in America since pre-Columbian times for flour and oil from its nutritious seeds. Valuable oil is now extracted from the seeds in the United States and Europe. Cultivated strains are bred to have large heads, and are all the same size and height for production and easy harvest. They track the sun from east to west each day, an entire field moving in unison; the common name refers to this trait, as does the Spanish name, Mirasol. The state flower of Kansas, the Sunflower blooms from June to September.

Identification A tall, coarse, leafy plant, commonly branched in the upper half; flower heads have a central maroon disk surrounded by many bright yellow rays. Height: 2–13′. Flower heads 3–5″ wide, with stiff scales among the tiny flowers; bracts around head broad, narrowing abruptly to a slender tip. Leaves 3–12″ long, the lowest heart-shaped or oval, pointed at the tip, with irregular teeth along the edges; upper leaves smaller, narrower.

Habitat Dry open plains and foothills, especially disturbed areas.

Range Much of North America.

48

Desert Marigold *Baileya multiradiata*

Beginning in late spring, miles of southwestern roads may be lined with the brilliant yellow of Desert Marigolds in display. In the garden, a single plant grows into a perfect hemisphere of yellow, blooming continuously throughout the heat of the summer and into the fall, requiring little care. The plants are toxic; the medicinal odor encourages grazing animals to avoid them, but when food is scarce, sheep may eat marigolds and be poisoned. Desert Marigold blooms from April to October.

Identification   Branched, woolly, grayish plants, leafy mostly in the lower half; many nearly leafless stalks, each bearing a brilliant yellow flower head. Height; 12–20″. Flower heads 1½–2″ wide, with 25–50 overlapping rays, toothed across a blunt tip; rays becoming papery after seed set, and persisting. Leaves covered with white wool; 1½–3″ long; oval and pinnately divided into several toothed or divided lobes. Fruit seedlike, without bristles or scales.

Habitat   Sandy or gravelly places in deserts; common along roads.

Range   SE. California to S. Utah and W. Texas, south to N. Mexico.

Brittlebush *Encelia farinosa*

In the spring, roadsides and hills of western Arizona and southern California are colored with massive, round clumps of the brilliant yellow Brittlebush. A member of the sunflower family, the plant is named for its brittle stems; when broken, they exude a fragrant resin. The dense, pale hairs on the leaves help to reflect the heat, keeping the leaves cool and allowing the plant to survive in hot deserts. Brittlebush blooms from March to June.

Identification Round, silvery-leaved shrubs with loose clusters of bright yellow flower heads held well above the foliage. Height: 3–5′. Flower heads 2–3″ across, each with 8–18 bright yellow rays surrounding a yellow central disk (dark brown in the southern part of its range); the tiny individual flowers of the disk enfolded to form a scale. Leaves 1¼–4″ long, broadest near the base and pointed at the tip; covered with silvery hairs.

Habitat Dry slopes, washes, and roadsides in the desert.

Range SE. California across S. Nevada to SW. Utah, W. Arizona, and NW. Mexico.

Heartleaf Arnica *Arnica cordifolia*

The bright yellow rays and yellow buttonlike center of the flower head unmistakably signal that the Heartleaf Arnica is a member of the daisy family. Species of *Arnica* extend around the Northern Hemisphere; of the nearly 20 species in the West, this is the only one with heart-shaped leaves, but in open areas the species may have narrower leaves without the notch at the base. Heartleaf Arnica blooms from May through August.

Identification   Stems in patches, with 2 or 3 pairs of heart-shaped leaves, topped by a single yellow flower head. Height: 4–24″. Flower head 2–3½″ wide, with 10–15 rays; the bracts at the base of the head with long, spreading hairs. Leaves heart-shaped, 1½–5″ long; those at the base on long stalks, those on the stem short-stalked or stalkless. Fruit seedlike, with a tuft of pale tan or white hairs on top.

Habitat   Lightly shaded or open areas in the mountains, sometimes along banks of roads.

Range   Alaska to New Mexico, westward nearly to the Pacific Coast; also in Michigan.

Blazing Star *Mentzelia laevicaulis*

After most other flowers are gone, the Blazing Star begins to bloom, its sharp, bright petals crowned by the soft radiance of its long stamens. This species belongs to the loasa, or stick-leaf, family, a small group confined almost entirely to the semiarid regions of the Americas. The waxy-looking, somewhat translucent petals and satiny white stems are characteristic of most members of the family. The Blazing Star flowers are open only from the late afternoon until early morning; they bloom from June to September.

Identification   Large, starlike lemon-yellow flowers on branches at the top of a stout, satiny white stem. Height: 1–3′. Flowers 2–5″ wide; petals 5, narrow, pointed; stamens numerous, 1 between each pair of petals with a broad, flat stalk. Leaves 4–12″ long; lance-shaped, irregularly lobed, and covered with tiny, barbed hairs. Fruit a capsule, maturing beneath the rest of the flower.

Habitat   Semiarid regions, on gravelly or sandy slopes or flats.

Range   SE. British Columbia to S. California, east to Montana, Wyoming, and Utah.

56

Monument Plant *Frasera speciosa*

On open mountain slopes there are two kinds of plants with stout main stems and broad oval leaves. One is this flower, the stately, sentinel-like Monument Plant. It is distinguishable by its large flowers nestled near the juncture of stem and leaf, each flower with four petal lobes. Its extremely poisonous look-alike is the False Hellebore (*Veratrum* spp.); a member of the lily family, it has small, densely clustered flowers with six petal-like parts on each flower. Monument Plant blooms from May into August.

Identification   Robust main stem with leaves in evenly spaced rings; flowers yellowish-green, spotted with purple. Height: 4–7′. Flowers 1–1½″ wide with 4 petal lobes joined at the base, and 4 stamens. Leaves 10–20″ long; broadly lance-shaped, 3–4 in a ring on the stout stem; evenly spaced and progressively smaller from the ground upward.

Habitat   Rich soil in woodland openings and on open mountain slopes, at middle to high elevations.

Range   E. Washington to central California and N. Mexico, and from Montana through the Rockies to W. Texas.

Klamath Weed *Hypericum perforatum*

First discovered in the United States in 1793, this aggressive immigrant from Europe is called Common St. Johnswort in the East. It appeared near the Klamath River in northern California about 1900, and spread very rapidly. The plant causes ulcerating sores in livestock that eat it; by 1940 it had made a quarter of a million acres of rangeland worthless. In 1945 two beetles were introduced from Europe, one to feed on the roots of this species and the other on the foliage; the balance achieved is a success story of biological control. Klamath Weed blooms from June to September.

Identification Stems branched and leafy, especially near the top, with bright yellow, starlike flowers in a round-topped cluster. Height: 1–3′. Flower a golden, 5-pointed star, about 1″ across; petals sometimes with black dots near the tips. Stamens many, clustered into 3–5 bunches. Leaves in pairs on the stem, ½–1½″ long; elliptical, with many tiny dark dots that are translucent when held to the light.

Habitat Roadsides and pastures.

Range Especially common from California to Washington.

60

Desert Plume *Stanleya pinnata*

The slender golden wands of flowers rising above the gray sagebrush belong to Desert Plume, also called Golden Prince's Plume. There are only a few species of *Stanleya* in the West; all are similar and easily recognized. Desert Plume is one of several plants whose presence indicates that the soil contains the toxic mineral selenium. Therefore when the great coal strip mines of the West are reclaimed, soils that once supported Desert Plume are not used. This species blooms from May to July.

Identification Tall stems with coarsely divided leaves and lacy wands of yellow flowers. Height: 1½–5′. Flowers with 4 petals, ⅜–⅝″ long, each densely hairy on the inner side of the brownish base. Leaves bluish-green, 2–6″ long; pinnately divided into a few narrow lobes. Fruit a pod, 1¼–2½″ long; on a slender stalk joined to a slightly thicker stalk.

Habitat Deserts and plains to the lower mountains; often with sagebrush, but also in open pine woods.

Range SE. Oregon to SE. California, east to W. Texas, and north to W. North Dakota.

62

Woolly Mullein *Verbascum thapsus*

Also called Common Mullein or Flannel Mullein, this ungainly member of the snapdragon family must have made it to North America in colonial times and then spread rapidly. In the West, it is also called Miner's Candle, from a gold miners' practice of dipping the stalks in tallow for torches; Greeks and Romans did the same. It has also been used to line moccasins, as tea, and as a treatment for a variety of ailments. As a weed, Woolly Mullein is everywhere; herbicides applied to the plants often cause the top of the stalk to take on a bizarre "cock's comb" shape. Woolly Mullein blooms from June to August.

Identification A spike resembling a pole, with the pale yellow flowers densely packed above the leafy stem. Height: 2–7'. Flowers scattered in a dense spike; each ¾–1" across; slightly bilateral, with 5 petal lobes. Leaves are oval and pointed; to 16" long, with feltlike hairs. Seeds minute, produced by the thousands.

Habitat Open places.

Range Virtually throughout North America.

64

Meadow Goldenrod *Solidago canadensis*

The appearance of the tall, handsome yellow plumes of the Meadow Goldenrod signals the waning of summer. The only similar plant in the West is Missouri Goldenrod (*S. missouriensis*), which is smaller, with smooth stems. Goldenrods are members of the sunflower family; the feathery yellow cluster atop the wandlike stem is actually composed of hundreds of tiny heads, each head structurally like that of a sunflower, but much smaller and with far fewer flowers. Meadow Goldenrod blooms from May through September, most prolifically in the later months.

Identification   Tall, finely hairy, leafy stems with tiny yellow flower heads on arching branches, in a long or flat-topped cluster. Height: 1–5′. Flowers clustered in heads about ⅛″ long, each head with 3 short rays. Leaves lance-shaped, 2–5″ long; finely hairy, with 3 prominent veins. Fruit seedlike, sparsely hairy, bearing numerous pale bristles on top.

Habitat   Meadows and open forest.

Range   Across Canada and in much of the United States.

White Sweet Clover *Melilotus alba*

White Sweet Clover has a multitude of tiny spires of pealike flowers over the entire plant. It often lines roads at lower elevations; its place is taken by Yellow Sweet Clover (*M. officinalis*) at slightly higher elevations. On a still day, sweet clovers will fill the air with a scent like that of new-mown hay. White Sweet Clover blooms from May through October.

Identification Coarse, tall plants with many spires of tiny, pealike white flowers; leaves divided into 3 segments. Height: 2–10′. Flowers pealike, less than ¼″ long, nodding in slender spires 1½–5″ long. Leaves divided into 3 segments ¾–1¼″ long, toothed along their edges. Fruit a small pod about ³⁄₁₆″ long, usually containing only 1 seed.

Habitat Along roadsides, in riverbeds, old fields, and wherever the ground has been disturbed.

Range Throughout North America; especially common from Washington to California.

Yarrow *Achillea millefolium*

A close inspection of the flower cluster, with its many tiny heads of flowers, will reveal that this species is a member of the sunflower family. From a distance, Yarrow resembles the Wild Carrot or Queen Anne's Lace (*Daucous carota*), a member of the carrot or parsley family. That species, however, has individual flowers rather than heads of flowers, and flower stalks joined to the same point at the top of the stem; the one central flower of the cluster is maroon. Yarrow, found nearly worldwide, has many names, among them Milfoil, Plumajillo ("little feather"), Sneezeweed, and Nosebleed. Yarrow blooms from March to October.

Identification   Aromatic, feathery leaves on a tough, fibrous stem, with a flattish cluster of small, white flower heads on top. Height: 12–40″. Individual flower heads with 3–5 broad, roundish rays, ⅛″ long, surrounding 10–30 tiny disk flowers. Leaves lance-shaped in outline, to 8″ long; repeatedly divided into very fine segments.

Habitat   Open areas from lowlands to mountains.

Range   Throughout most of temperate North America.

Spectacle Pod *Dithyrea wislizenii*

The Spectacle Pod, a member of the mustard family, gets its name from its fruits—many little green pods that, when mature, resemble eyeglasses. Technically the pod is like that of other mustards, divided into two cells by a parchmentlike partition. In this species, however, the typically long pod has become very short and flat, the parchment forming the seam between each of the spectacle's "lenses." There are only two species of *Dithyrea;* the California Spectacle Pod (*D. californica*) ranges farther west and has shallowly lobed, yellowish-green leaves. Spectacle Pod blooms from February to May, and often again after summer rains.

Identification   A grayish-hairy plant with pinnately lobed leaves; dense white flowers produce flat, twin-lobed pods. Height: 6–24″. Flowers with 4 white petals about ½″ long. Basal leaves to 6″ long; the edges deeply and pinnately lobed; stem leaves shorter and less deeply lobed. Fruit matures into a flat pod nearly ½″ wide.

Habitat   Open sandy soil in arid grassland and deserts.

Range   W. Oklahoma and W. Texas to S. Utah and W. Arizona.

72

Blue Yucca *Yucca baccata*

A multitude of yuccas grows in the Southwest, and one species is the state flower of New Mexico. For pollination, they are highly dependent on a small moth, which can often be found inside the flowers. In turn, the moth is dependent on the yucca, for its larvae consume a portion of the young seeds the parent helped produce. This plant is sometimes called Banana Yucca or Datil. Yuccas bloom mostly in the spring and early summer, the Blue Yucca from April to July.

Identification Rigid, spine-tipped leaves in 1 or several rosettes, and a long cluster of large whitish flowers on a stalk about as tall as the leaves. Height: 2½–5′. Flowers 2–4″ long; hanging from branches of the main stalk, with 6 petal-like segments. Leaves swordlike, to 3′ long. Pod fleshy, hanging, cylindrical, 2½–10″ long.

Habitat Rocky soil in deserts, grasslands, brushy areas, or dry, open woods.

Range SE. California, S. Nevada, and Utah to SW. Colorado, south to W. Texas, New Mexico, Arizona, and into Mexico.

Kinnikinnick *Arctostaphylos uva-ursi*

The tiny lantern-shaped flowers signify that this is a member of the heath family. Kinnikinnick is found in cool regions throughout much of the Northern Hemisphere, and because of its wide range and usefulness to early peoples, it must have a hundred names. A common one is Bearberry, for bears and other wildlife relish its fruit. Kinnikinnick has smooth red bark, like the related manzanitas, which are plentiful in the brushlands of California. Kinnikinnick blooms from March to June.

Identification A low, matted plant with smooth red-brown stems, leathery oval leaves, and small, pale pink or white, lanternlike flowers. Height: A creeper about 6″ tall. Flowers hanging, about ¼″ long with 5 small, curled lobes around the narrow opening. Leaves dark green, leathery, oval; ¼–1¼″ long. Fruit a red berry, ⅜″ wide.

Habitat Open places near the Pacific Coast; also open woods high in most of the western mountains.

Range Coastal N. California to Alaska; east from Oregon and Washington to the Rockies of W. Montana, south to New Mexico.

76

White Heather *Cassiope mertensiana*

Members of the heath family, heathers are humble but showy relatives of the rhododendron and azalea, and also the manzanita, which forms part of the dense, flammable brush called chaparral in California. Heathers are small shrubs with short, needlelike leaves; these plants are characteristic of cold, wet areas. In the West, two other heathers are common: Pink Mountain Heather (*Phyllodoce empetriformis*) has bright pink, bell-like flowers; Brewer's Mountain Heather (*P. breweri*) is similar but has stamens longer than the petals. White Mountain Heather blooms from June through August.

Identification A matted plant with short, needlelike leaves; flowers like tiny white bells hang from slender stalks near the tips of branches. Height: 2–12″. Flowers about ¼″ long; with 5 blunt lobes gently curling back around the rim. Leaves very narrow, ⅛–¼″ long; borne opposite one another, and arranged in 4 rows, nearly hiding the stem.

Habitat Open slopes and among rocks at and above timberline.

Range Alaska and Canada south to central California, N. Nevada, and W. Montana.

78

Southwestern Thornapple *Datura wrightii*

Parts of this plant and some of its relatives in the potato or tomato family are dangerously toxic, often lethal. Carefully administered, they have been used as anesthetics and narcotics since before recorded history. Large, funnel-shaped white or pale violet flowers and round, spiny fruits characterize the genus. Jimsonweed (*D. stramonium*) is a close relative; its fruit has many small spines and does not hang, and the flower is only about three inches long. Southwestern Thornapple blooms from May to November, its large flowers lasting only one night.

Identification Large, trumpet-shaped white flowers protrude from coarse, rank-smelling foliage. Height: 1–5′. Flowers 6″ long; rim has 5 slender teeth. Leaves oval, pointed, to 6″ long. Fruit spherical, 1½″ long, hangs down; covered by spines less than ½″ long.

Habitat Loose sand in gullies and on plains.

Range Central California east to Texas and south into Mexico.

Sego Lily *Calochortus nuttallii*

Calochortus comes from the Greek for "beautiful grass." Nearly 60 species, some very rare and protected, grow only in North America. The genus, sometimes called "mariposa tulip," is easily recognized, but identification of a species requires close attention to details of the gland at each petal base. The Sego Lily's edible bulb is credited with saving the lives of early Utah settlers, certainly influencing the selection of this species as the state flower. It blooms from May to July.

Identification Erect, unbranched stems with few leaves, topped by 1–4 bell-shaped white flowers in an open cluster. Height: 6–18″. Flowers 1–2″ wide with 3 broad, fan-shaped petals, yellow around the gland at the base and marked with reddish-brown or purple above the gland. Gland circular, surrounded by a fringed membrane. Leaves 2–4″ long, narrow, with uprolled edges.

Habitat Dry plains, among sagebrush, and open pine forest.

Range E. Montana and W. North Dakota to E. Idaho and NW. Nebraska, across Utah and W. Colorado to N. Arizona and NW. New Mexico.

Western Wake Robin *Trillium ovatum*

The Wake Robin, or Trillium, blooms in forests, at about the time the robin arrives from its southern winter stay. This species and other trilliums are lilies; the leaves, sepals, petals, and parts of the ovary occur in rings of three, giving the genus name. There are few species in the West, all with the distinctive ring of three broad leaves: Klamath Trillium (*T. rivale*), Giant Wake Robin (*T. chloropetalum*), and Roundleaf Trillium (*T. petiolatum*). All are early bloomers; the Western Wake Robin flowers from February to June.

Identification White flower on a stalk with a ring of 3 oval, bluntly pointed leaves. Height: 4–16″. Flowers 1½–3″ wide, the 3 white petals becoming pink with age. Leaves broad, 2–8″ long, without stalks at base.

Habitat Banks of streams and the floor of open or deep woods.

Range British Columbia and Alberta to central California and NW. Colorado.

Bunchberry *Cornus canadensis*

This humble ground cover is a close relative of the magnificent Western Dogwood (*C. nuttallii*). Bunchberry is one of the smallest members of the dogwood family. It spreads by nearly horizontal rootstocks and occurs in patches, making it a fine ground cover. It is equally attractive in flower or fruit. The tiny flowers are not at all showy, but they are surrounded by clear white bracts. The buttonlike central cluster of flowers matures into a tight bunch of bright red berries that last for some time. Bunchberry blooms from June to August.

Identification Low, leafy patches; stems topped by a dense cluster of brownish flowers, surrounded by 4 bright white or pale pink bracts. Height: 2–8″. Flower cluster (from bract tip to bract tip) to 4″ across; small flowers in center have 4 petals and 4 sepals. Leaves broadest near the middle, pointed, ¾–3″ long. Fruit a red berry, in tight clusters.

Habitat Moist woods.

Range Across the North; south along the Pacific Coast and in mountains to N. California, Idaho, and N. New Mexico; also in the East.

86

Queen's Cup *Clintonia uniflora*

The pure white flowers, shaped like a broad bell, give a second common name for this species—Bride's Bonnet. This flower is a member of the lily family. It usually occurs in open woods, spreading in semi-shaded spots, forming patches of shiny leaves sprinkled with starlike flowers. As the season matures, the flowers of Queen's Cup form a single blue berry. Queen's Cup blooms from May to July.

Identification A single, starlike white flower (rarely 2) on a short, leafless stalk that grows from a cluster of 2 or 3 shiny, elliptic leaves. Height: 2½–6″. Flowers 1–1½″ across, the 6 segments forming a broad bell. Leaves 2½–6″ long. Fruit a lustrous blue berry, ¼–½″ across; at the top of the flower stalk in July and August.

Habitat Coniferous forests, often in moist areas.

Range Alaska to N. California and inland to the southern Sierra Nevada, east to E. Oregon and W. Montana.

Long-leaved Phlox *Phlox longifolia*

Western North America is the region where most of the members of the phlox family are found. Species of *Phlox* can usually be recognized by the broad, flat petal lobes, joined almost at right angles to a very narrow tube. The flowers are usually white, pink, or pale lilac—sometimes all colors in one area—and when in full bloom may cover the plant so completely as to obscure the foliage. Long-leaved Phlox blooms from April to July.

Identification Slender stems in clumps, with loose clusters of bright pink, pale lilac, or chalky-white flowers. Height: 4–16″. Flower nearly T-shaped when viewed from the side; about 1″ across; petals joined, forming lobes, with tips free; style at center of the flower has 3 short, threadlike branches atop ovary; the slender tube ½–¾″ long. Translucent membranes, folded outward, between the narrow green lobes of the calyx. Leaves paired, up to 3″ long; very narrow.

Habitat Dry, open, rocky places from low to moderate elevations.

Range S. British Columbia to S. California, east to the Rockies from New Mexico to W. Montana.

Western Pasqueflower *Anemone occidentalis*

"Pasque," from an old French word for Easter, refers to this plant's early flowering and to the purity of its white flower. It is also called Mountain Pasqueflower, for its evident preference for mountain slopes and windswept ridges. In early song and legend of Native Americans, the species was a herald of spring; its shaggy silvery head of feathery seeds also made it a symbol of old age. A similar species with pale blue flowers, *A. patens*, is the state flower of South Dakota. Western Pasqueflower blooms from May to September.

Identification   A hairy plant with finely divided leaves and stems with 1 white or cream flower at the tip. Height: 8–24″. Flowers 1¼–2″ wide; petal-like sepals hairy on the back; there are no true petals. Leaves 1½–3″ wide; finely divided into narrow, crowded segments; several leaves at base and 3 in a ring beneath the flowers. Fruit a shaggy, silvery head of feathery plumes, each with a seedlike base.

Habitat   Mountain slopes and meadows.

Range   British Columbia to the Sierra Nevada, east to NE. Oregon and W. Montana.

Prickly Poppy *Argemone polyanthemos*

This thistlelike plant belongs to the poppy family, unlike true thistles, which are members of the sunflower family. It has latex-laden sap, which usually indicates that a plant is distasteful, or, as in this species, toxic. The spines of the Prickly Poppy, therefore, may serve as a first warning to livestock; the bad taste is a second; and the toxin is the final lesson to the animal that does not heed. The seeds are also toxic. Other prickly poppies in the West may have white, pinkish, or pale lavender petals. This one blooms from April to July.

Identification Tall, pale blue-green, prickly plants with large white flowers. Height: 1½–4′. Flowers about 3″ wide, with 4–6 slightly crumpled petals. Stamens form a round yellow "button" in the center. Buds with 2 or 3 sepals, each with a stout "horn" ¼–⅝″ long, dropping off as the flower opens. Fruit a capsule, splitting open at the top; largest spines lack prickles at base.

Habitat Sandy or gravelly soil on plains or brushy slopes.

Range South Dakota and E. Wyoming through to central Texas and south-central New Mexico.

94

Claret Cup Cactus *Echinocereus triglochidiatus*

Clusters of low, cylindrical stems covered by scarlet flowers immediately identify this handsome species. Its beautiful, long-lasting red flowers are unique in the United States, making it very popular for desert landscaping. Its popularity has earned it several names, such as King's Cup Cactus and Strawberry Cactus. A word of caution: the Claret Cup Cactus and many other cacti are now protected by law in most states. Some are in danger of extinction; to dig them may result in stiff fines. It is best to buy cacti from reputable retailers. Claret Cup Cactus blooms from June to August.

Identification Cup-shaped bright red flowers with many petals on top of spiny, cylindrical stems. Height: 2–16″. Flowers 1¼–2″ wide, with many petals. There may be as few as 2 or 3 stout spines in a cluster or as many as 16 very slender, needlelike ones.

Habitat Rocky desert slopes, among brush, or in dry mountain woodlands.

Range SE. California to S. Utah and Colorado, south to W. Texas and N. Mexico.

Orange Agoseris *Agoseris aurantiaca*

In the western mountains, this is one of the very few orange-flowered members of the huge sunflower family. The head is made up of tiny flowers, each with a petal-like strap on one side; this arrangement reveals that it is a close relative of the Common Dandelion, as does the milky sap of the stem. In fact, there are several yellow-flowered species of *Agoseris* that are called Mountain Dandelion. Orange Agoseris is also related to Chicory. This species flowers in July and August.

Identification   Many small, coppery-orange flowers in a head about 1″ wide; slender stem; all leaves at the base. Height: 4–24″. Flowers tiny, in a head with several long-tapered bracts forming a deep cup around the base. Leaves 2–14″ long; narrow, broadest above the middle, usually with a few prominent teeth along the edges. Fruit seedlike, with a stalk at tip about as long as the body; topped by 50 or more fine silvery bristles.

Habitat   Meadows and grassy areas in mountain forests.

Range   W. Canada to N. California and New Mexico.

Desert Paintbrush *Castilleja chromosa*

The paintbrushes are classic western wildflowers. Their brilliant color, red in most, lavender or cream in a few, comes from the calyx and upper leaflike bracts; the rest of the flower is small and beaklike. Paintbrushes may attach their roots to those of another plant and steal its nutrients. As a group, paintbrushes are easy to identify, but the species are notoriously difficult. Desert Paintbrush blooms from April to August.

Identification	Several erect stems with a few ragged, brushlike, bright orange or red tips. Height: 4–16″. Bracts and calyx red or orange; the calyx deeply cleft above and below, shallowly cleft on each side, resulting in 4 bluntly pointed lobes. Petals modified into a bilateral, beaklike structure, ¾–1¼″ long; upper lip projecting, lower forming a small green bump. Leaves 1–2″ long; lower ones very narrow, the upper divided into 3 or 5 very narrow lobes.
Habitat	Dry, open soil, often with sagebrush.
Range	E. Oregon, S. Idaho, and central Wyoming to E. California, N. Arizona, NW. New Mexico, and central Colorado.

100

Golden-beard Penstemon *Penstemon barbatus*

In midsummer, hillsides in the Southwest may be covered with tubular red flowers, a favorite source of nectar for hummingbirds. All have the same general form, and one must look closely to make an accurate identification. Most of the red penstemons have strongly bilateral flowers, but on one, the Scarlet Bugler (*P. centranthifolius*), they are nearly radial, and that species may be confused with the unrelated Skyrocket (*Ipomopsis aggregata*). In most areas, Golden-beard Penstemon has yellow hairs near the opening of the flower. It blooms from June to September.

Identification	Flowers bright red, bilateral, tubular; spreading in an open cluster at the top of a stem with a few paired leaves. Height: 1–3′. Flowers 1–1½″ long; upper lip projecting forward like a visor; 3-lobed lower lip bent down. Stamens 5; 4 fertile, 1 sterile. Leaves gray-green, narrow; 2–5″ long; paired on the stem, smooth.
Habitat	Dry, rocky slopes in open forests.
Range	S. Colorado to Arizona and W. Texas, south into Mexico.

Striped Coral Root *Corallorhiza striata*

This orchid is called a saprophyte because it lacks chlorophyll. Therefore, unlike most plants, it is not green and cannot use the sun's energy to make sugar from carbon dioxide. Instead it relies on dissolved nutrients in the rich organic matter of the duff it grows in. Beneath the surface of the ground is a tangled mass of rootlike stems, which may lie dormant for one or several seasons, storing nutrients. Like most orchids, the Striped Coral Root has a singularly different lower lip; this lip starts out as an upper petal, and the flower rotates exactly one-half turn as it develops. Striped Coral Root blooms from May to August.

Identification Flesh-colored stems, alone or in clusters, with a spire of pale pink, brown-striped flowers. Height: 6–20″. Flowers bilateral, about 1″ wide, with 5 similar petal-like parts, and 1 lower petal, spoonlike near the tip. Leaves reduced to scales on the stem.

Habitat Deep, shady woods.

Range Canada to Mexico.

Skyrocket *Ipomopsis aggregata*

The name Skyrocket is apt for this open flower cluster, five feet tall and truly resembling an exploding rocket of red streamers and bursts. It grows readily from seed and is a handsome addition to the native garden. Some populations of Skyrocket in the Southwest produce progressively paler flowers as the season matures, especially when hummingbirds—among the main pollinators—have moved higher in the mountains or northward. Then nocturnal moths, which can see the paler flowers, become important pollinators. Also known as Desert Trumpet, Scarlet Gilia, and Skunk Flower, this species blooms from May to September.

Identification   Open clusters of trumpet-shaped bright red or pink flowers with 5 petal points. Height: 6–84″. Flower a 5-pointed star attached to a narrow tube; ¾–1¼″ long. Leaves mostly at the base; 1–2″ long; pinnately divided into narrow segments.

Habitat   Dry slopes from sagebrush to open forest.

Range   E. Oregon to W. North Dakota, south to S. California, N. Mexico, and W. Texas.

106

Scarlet Globemallow *Sphaeralcea coccinea*

Across the landscape of the West, a splash of bright red-orange signals the presence of one of the many species of globemallow. Their five petals and "shaving brush" cluster of stamens make the group easily recognizable, although the individual species are troublesome even for the professional botanist. As the common name indicates, these plants belong to the mallow family. Scarlet Globemallow blooms from April to August.

Identification	Low plants with velvety-hairy, roundish, lobed leaves; flowers brick- or orange-red, single or in clusters. Height: 5–20″. Flowers with 5 petals; many clustered stamens. Leaves ¾–2″ wide; rounded, divided into 3 broad or narrow, divided or toothed lobes. Fruit a capsule, splitting into 10–14 wedge-shaped segments, about ⅛″ long.
Habitat	Open ground in arid grasslands; pinyon-juniper woodlands.
Range	Central Canada to W. Montana, Utah, NE. Arizona, and New Mexico, east to Texas and Iowa.

Woods' Rose *Rosa woodsii*

This is one of several wild roses (sometimes called "species roses") that occur in the West. Wild roses have only five to seven petals; through centuries of painstaking hybridizing, rose lovers have created an enormous variety of flowers, some with hundreds of petals, to delight the gardener. All our modern roses are descended from wild ancestors like this one. The fruits, called hips, are rich in vitamin C, and the seeds are rich in vitamin E. Woods' Rose blooms from April to September.

Identification A thorny shrub with bright pink or white flowers; sometimes bristly. Height: 4–6′. Flowers sweet-scented, 2–3″ wide; with 5 broad petals and many stamens. Sepals have glands on the margins. Stems have stout prickles. Leaves blue-green, pinnately compound, with 5–7 ovate leaflets; 1¼″ long; sharply toothed on edges.

Habitat Woods and open places in the mountains.

Range British Columbia to Alberta, south to S. California, W. Texas, and N. Mexico, and east to Ontario and Missouri.

Farewell to Spring *Clarkia amoena*

As the lush green grass of spring starts to turn gold in the summer heat, the poppy-shaped flowers of Farewell to Spring begin to appear. They often grow together in throngs, coloring wide swaths of hillside. The four petals may be pink or have a reddish-purple blotch; they and the ovary beneath indicate that this species is a member of the primrose family. Most species of the genus grow in California; all are reddish-pink or darker, and some are very rare. Farewell to Spring blooms from June to August.

Identification	Slender open annual plants; showy cup-shaped pink flowers, in a loose cluster. Height: 6–36″. Flowers ¾–1½″ long, with 4 fan-shaped petals; evenly pink or with reddish-purple central blotch. Four reddish sepals, twisted to the side, remaining attached at tips. Leaves lance-shaped, ¾–3″ long.
Habitat	Drying grassy slopes and openings in brush and woods.
Range	S. British Columbia to central California.

Threadleaf Phacelia *Phacelia linearis*

After a winter of ample moisture, open, drying areas may be carpeted with the reddish-lavender Threadleaf Phacelia. It is a member of a very large genus of about 200 species, most in the West. As with this species, they have their flowers in a coil that unfurls slowly, the open flowers always on the top, their new buds tucked in the center. Only two plant families in the West have such a flower cluster: the waterleaf family (to which this plant belongs), and the equally common borago family. Threadleaf Phacelia blooms from April to June.

Identification Flowers reddish lavender, in loose coils on slender, usually branched stems. Height: 4–20″. Flowers broadly bell-shaped, with 5 round lobes at rim. Leaves narrowly lance-shaped, ½–4″ long, hairy; sometimes with 1–4 pairs of small lobes in the lower half.

Habitat Among brush and in open, grassy areas, in foothills and on plains.

Range S. British Columbia to N. California, east across Utah and Idaho to W. Wyoming.

Bindweed *Convolvulus arvensis*

The pretty little funnel-shaped flowers of this aggressive and unwelcome Eurasian immigrant are typical of the morning glory family. The plant's deep roots, difficult to extract, simply produce more plants when broken or scattered. *Convolvulus* is Latin for "entwined" and refers to the twining habit of the stems. To the farmer, the name may seem appropriate because of the plant's tendency to tangle around the drive shafts of farm machinery. Garden morning glories are in the genus *Ipomoea*, differing from *Convolvulus* in certain technical features. Bindweed blooms from May to October.

Identification Flowers white, small, funnel-like, barely lifted above the twining stems and triangular leaves. Height: Less than 6″ on the ground; may climb to a height of more than 10′. Flowers funnel-like, about 1″ long and wide. Leaves ¾–1½″ long; triangular or arrow-shaped. Fruit a small, spherical capsule, usually containing 4 black seeds.

Habitat Roadsides, fields, and agricultural areas.

Range Nearly throughout North America.

Bitterroot *Lewisia rediviva*

This ground-hugging, spectacular succulent is the state flower of Montana. Its scientific name honors Meriwether Lewis of the Lewis and Clark expedition; *rediviva* means "brought to life." The plant flourishes in barren, clay ground, and when dug and pressed for a specimen, remains alive for weeks or months, often regenerating from seemingly dried and dead roots. Bitterroot, also called Sandrose (and "Spatlum" by the indigenous peoples of Oregon), blooms from March through June.

Identification Flowers almost on the ground; deep pink to nearly white with 12–18 petals. Leaves succulent, very narrow. Height: 2″ or less. Flowers 1–1¼″ wide, with 12–18 petals; sepals only 6–8. Leaves in a rosette, ½–2″ long; very narrow and nearly cylindrical. Fruit a small capsule with dark, round, shiny seeds.

Habitat Open areas among sagebrush or pines.

Range British Columbia to S. California, east to Montana and Colorado.

Moss Pink *Silene acaulis*

This member of the pink, or carnation, family has the technical features of its genus, but it has developed in response to the freezing, drying winds of its high, rocky habitat. The stems are dwarfed, huddled together for protection, and the plant looks like a moss. Studded with brilliant pink flowers, this attractive alpine cushion plant resembles two other unrelated species: Purple Saxifrage (*Saxifraga oppositifolia*), which has oval, pointed leaves and only two styles in the center of the flower; and *Phlox*, which has the petals joined into a very slender tube. Moss Pink blooms from June to August.

Identification Thick, mosslike mats with bright pink flowers. Height: 1–2½″; mats up to 1′ wide. Flowers about ½″ wide; the 5 petals notched at the tip with very slender bases attached to the inside base of the tubular calyx; 3 threadlike styles atop the ovary. Leaves ¼–⅝″ long; very narrow and paired.

Habitat Moist areas above timberline, often in rock crevices.

Range In mountains of Canada, Oregon, N. Arizona, N. New Mexico, and New Hampshire.

120

Desert Four O'Clock *Mirabilis multiflora*

This plant belongs to the four o'clock family, which includes the garden favorite Common Four O'Clock (*M. jalapa*) and Bougainvillea, a popular climbing ornamental from Brazil. Desert Four O'Clock, as its name implies, begins to bloom as the heat of the day subsides. As the following morning begins to warm, the flowers close forever, and a new set will open as the cycle repeats. The Desert Four O'Clock blooms from April through September.

Identification   Broadly tubular, vibrant pink flowers bloom in the evening from five-lobed cups; leaves heart-shaped or broadly oval and bluntly pointed. Height: 1–2′. Flowers fragile, tubular, about 1″ wide and 2″ long, the stamens protruding. A large, blackish, stonelike fruit forms at the base of each flower, inside the 5-toothed cup. Plants are often bushy; leaves, 1–4″ long, paired along the stem.

Habitat   Common in open areas among juniper and pinyon trees, extending onto grasslands and into the deserts.

Range   S. California to S. Colorado and W. Texas, south into N. Mexico.

Desert Sand Verbena *Abronia villosa*

After a winter of ample rains, Desert Sand Verbena, a member of the four o'clock family, may carpet the desert in a continuous swath of pink for mile upon mile. White- or yellow-flowered species also occur, but *Abronia* is always easily recognized by the round heads and a swelling at the base of each flower that encloses the ovary. The swelling enlarges as the shiny, seedlike black fruit matures, eventually to be tumbled by the wind to new places. Desert Sand Verbena blooms from March to October.

Identification A soft-haired, sticky plant with trumpet-shaped, bright pink flowers in heads that bloom on stalks growing from the angle formed by the leaf and stem. Height: Flower stalks to 10″ on trailing stems reaching 4′. Flower head 2–3″ wide; flared end with 5 lobes. Leaves ½–1½″ long; paired on the stem, oval but bluntly pointed, the edges slightly scalloped. Fruit ½″ long, with 3–5 wings.

Habitat Sandy deserts.

Range SE. California, S. Nevada, W. Arizona, and NW. Mexico.

124

Lewis' Monkeyflower *Mimulus lewisii*

Lewis' Monkeyflower is a striking plant of high mountain streams and springs. Its deep pink to reddish flowers are very likely to attract hummingbirds during their summer stay in the mountains. "Monkeyflower" refers to the impish "face" of some species in the group. The genus is very large, about half the species occurring in the varied habitats of California. Many are diminutive annuals; all have charming, colorful flowers ranging from yellow through pink, orange, or red, the colors often combined in harlequin fashion. Lewis' Monkeyflower blooms from June through August.

Identification   Showy, bilateral, deep pink to reddish flowers bloom in profusion at the tops of stems with paired leaves. Height: 1–3′. Flowers 1¼–2″ long; bilateral, with 3 lobes bent down and 2 bent upward near an opening marked with yellow hairs and dark violet lines. Leaves paired, 1–4″ long; toothed or plain on the edges.

Habitat   Wet, open places in the mountains.

Range   W. Canada to the S. Sierra Nevada, and to the higher mountains of Utah, Wyoming, and Montana.

126

Calypso *Calypso bulbosa*

When you espy this delightful little wildflower in the mottled woodland light, your first thought will be "orchid." The orchid family—a group of primarily tropical, tree-dwelling plants—boasts more members than any other family; but in all the world there is only one *Calypso* species. Its presence indicates that the woods are relatively old and undisturbed, for it requires a thick, rich duff. Orchids do not transplant well—if you find an orchid, leave it in peace, for its seed is needed in the wild. Calypso blooms from March to July.

Identification A single bilateral pink flower hangs from a slender stalk, with a single leaf on the ground at its base. Height: 3–8″. Flower about 1¼″ long; 2 petals and 3 similar sepals spread outward and upward; and 1 petal, the lip, divided into a spoonlike white tip with red-purple spots and a 2-lobed base with red-purple stripes. A single broad leaf, near the ground, 1¼–2½″ long, more or less plaited.

Habitat Thick duff and mossy ground in woods.

Range From N. California, NE. Arizona, and S. New Mexico through much of the North.

128

Few-flowered Shooting Star *Dodecatheon pulchellum*

The open cluster of dartlike flowers—points angled outward, colorful "tails" inward—resemble miniature firework displays. Shooting stars belong to the primrose family; a few species have white flowers, but about ten in the West are pink-flowered. All are easy to distinguish as shooting stars; technical features separate species. This plant blooms from April to August.

Identification   A few flowers resembling deep pink darts point in all directions from an open cluster atop a long, erect stalk. Height: 4–24″. Flowers ¾–1″ long; with 4–5 petal lobes sharply bent back; yellowish ring, usually with purplish lines, at base of lobes. Stamens form the point of the "dart," with smooth or slightly wrinkled tube joining them to the base of the petal lobes. Tip of the dart (stigma) barely broader than stalk. Leaves, all at the base, 2–16″ long; with smooth edges or small teeth.

Habitat   From coastal prairies to mountain meadows and streamsides.

Range   Throughout the West, to Wisconsin, Missouri, and N. Mexico.

130

Fireweed *Epilobium angustifolium*

Great pink spires of flowers identify Fireweed, a member
of the evening primrose family. For it to occur in great
patches usually means disaster has befallen other plants;
Fireweed likes open, disturbed areas, such as might
result from a devastating fire. It is also found along roads
and trails, or on riverbanks scoured by high water.
However, huge stands of the species slowly dwindle as
other plants begin to occupy the site in a progression
known as ecological succession. Also called the Great
Willow Herb, Fireweed blooms from June to September.

Identification Tall spires of pink flowers; leafy stems; often in dense
patches. Height: 2–7′. Flowers about 1″ wide, with 4
petals, narrow at base and broadly rounded above.
Leaves lance-shaped, 4–6″ long; veins forming loops
near the edges.

Habitat Disturbed soil in open, cool places; frequent along
highways and in burned areas from the lowlands well
into the mountains.

Range Throughout much of North America.

132

Hairy Vetch *Vicia villosa*

This species originated in Europe and Asia, but is naturalized in North America. Vetches are members of the pea family, climbing by coiling tendrils on the ends of the leaves. Sweet Peas and their wild relatives (*Lathyrus*) also have tendrils, but the tip of the style has hairs that make it resemble a little toothbrush; in vetches the style looks more like a shaving brush. Hairy Vetch and others have been introduced as valued green fodder and, like other members of the family, has bacteria in the roots that add nitrogen to the soil. Hairy Vetch blooms from May to July.

Identification Climbing plants covered with soft hairs; with clinging, coiling tendrils at ends of leaves, and long clusters of crowded, pealike, reddish-lavender or blue with white flowers. Height: 4–7′. Flowers 20–70, crowded, ½–¾″ long. Leaves pinnately compound, with 19–29 leaflets, each ¾–1½″ long. Fruit a pod, about ¾″ long.

Habitat On banks of roads, along fences, and in old fields.

Range Throughout much of North America.

Purple Loco *Oxytropis lambertii*

The name loco is given to about 300 species in the genera *Oxytropis* and *Astragalus;* some are extremely toxic and cause bizarre behavior in livestock. When range conditions are poor, hungry animals eat what they can find; those that eat loco can even become "hooked." Locos belong to the pea family; in *Oxytropis*, the keel is pointed, but in *Astragalus* it is not. Purple Loco blooms from June to September.

Identification Silvery, tufted plants with dense spires of pealike, bright reddish-lavender flowers held on long stalks just above the foliage. Height: 4–16″. Flowers upcurved, ½–1″ long; pealike in general form. Leaves pinnately divided; the individual lance-shaped segments ¼–1½″ long. Hairs joined to leaf by middle, like tiny teeter-totters (may be visible with a lens). Fruit an upward-pointing pod, ¾–1¼″ long, with groove on side against stem.

Habitat Plains, open areas in pine forests; often along roads.

Range Great Plains from Canada to Texas, west to the eastern base of the Rockies in Montana and Wyoming, and mountains of central Utah and Arizona.

136

Rydberg's Penstemon *Penstemon rydbergii*

The enthusiast, beginner or practiced, can immediately recognize the genus *Penstemon* by the paired, smooth leaves, bilateral flowers, and five stamens, one of which is always sterile. These flowers are also called "beard tongues" because this sterile fifth stamen is often bearded at the tip. The genus contains over 200 species, almost all of them only in the West. Identification to species is not difficult, but the sheer size of the group prohibits full representation in any guidebook; suffice Rydberg's to represent blue-flowered penstemons in the West. It blooms in June and July.

Identification   Small, bilateral, dark blue-violet flowers form 1 or more dense rings atop a stalk bearing paired leaves. Height: 8–24″. Flower ½–¾″ long, narrowly funnel-shaped; 2 upper lobes project forward, 3 lower lobes spread downward; hairy near the opening on the lower inside. Stamens 5, 1 with bearded tip. Leaves paired, lance-shaped, 1½–3″.

Habitat   Open mountain slopes.

Range   E. Washington to E. California, east to N. Arizona, Colorado, Wyoming, and SW. Montana.

138

Elephant Heads *Pedicularis groenlandica*

It takes only a glance at these flowers in their slender pink spires to know you have found Elephant Heads, also called Little Red Elephants. The petals form a perfect little pachyderm's forehead, trunk, and ears. This structure and unusual arrangement facilitates pollination and reduces the chance of hybridization with other species—the pollen is quite precisely placed on the insect. The similar Little Elephant Heads (*P. attolens*) is marked with white and rose and is not so perfectly elephantine—its "trunk," raised as if trumpeting, is only as long as the lower lip. Elephant Heads bloom from June through August.

Identification   Spires of deep pink flowers, like little elephant heads, held above sharply divided leaves. Height: 6–28″. Flowers about ½″ long (exclusive of the "trunk"). Leaves 2–10″ long; narrow, pinnately divided into sharp-toothed lobes.

Habitat   Wet meadows and small, cold streams.

Range   Throughout the western mountains and across boreal forests of North America; also along Atlantic Coast.

140

Fringe Cups *Tellima grandiflora*

Compared to large, brightly colored wildflowers, these plants have a subtle beauty from a distance. Their narrow, cream-colored spires of small flowers above the round cluster of foliage are graceful, but only close examination will reveal their unexpected delicacy and beauty of form. The cup at the base of the flower helps to distinguish this as a member of the saxifrage family, many of which are small inhabitants of shaded woods, but there is only one species of *Tellima*. Fringe Cups do well in the woodland garden; they bloom from April to July.

Identification   Spirelike wands of small cream or pinkish flowers with fringed petals above a cluster of roundish, lobed and scalloped leaves. Height: 12–32″. Flowers about ½″ wide, arranged along a slender stalk. Petals cleft along the edge and across the end into a curled fringe; usually cream-colored, but sometimes pinkish. Leaves 1–4″ wide; roundish, lobed and scalloped; basal leaves long-stalked.

Habitat   Moist places in woods.

Range   Alaska to coastal central California, east to Idaho.

142

Rocky Mountain Bee Plant *Cleome serrulata*

In late summer, this relative of the edible caper lines roads and covers expanses of rangeland with a blanket of pink. The flowers produce copious nectar, attracting bees (and giving rise to the common name). Also called Stinkweed, these plants have a skunklike odor and a bitter taste; but proper cooking removes the bitterness, and the greens were once a staple of Native Americans and early settlers. Tortillas made from the nearly unpalatable but nutritious seeds nurtured early Southwesterners through difficult drought. Rocky Mountain Bee Plant blooms from July to October.

Identification   Usually tall; flowers pink with 4 petals; leaves divided into 3 leaflets. Height: ½–7′. Flowers about ½″ long; 4 petals, each tapered to a very long, slender base; with 6 stamens, about twice as long as petals. Leaves with 3 leaflets, each ½–3″ long. Fruit a capsule on a long stalk.

Habitat   Plains, rangeland, roadsides, dry watercourses, and hillsides.

Range   E. Washington to N. California; east on Great Plains and south to Arizona, New Mexico, and Texas.

144

Teasel *Dipsacus sylvestris*

Teasels and their garden relatives, pincushions (*Scabiosa*), are immigrants from a family originally restricted to the Old World. Teasels were one of the few tools taken directly from nature. One species, Fuller's Teasel (*D. fullonum*), has small, hooked bracts in the head; it was used to "tease" and raise the nap on cloth. The distinctive heads make the genus easy to recognize. Teasel blooms from April to September, the first flowers in the head forming a ring around the equator, later ones blooming above and below so that two rings of flowers are ultimately present—a unique pattern.

Identification   Angular, prickly stems end in oval heads with many small, sharp bracts and small, tubular, pale purple flowers. Height: 1½–7'. Flower heads oval, 1¼–2" wide; many small, pointed bracts, each associated with a flower; beneath the head are a few large, upcurved bracts. Leaves to 1' long; lance-shaped, paired and joined at the stem; prickly on midvein on underside.

Habitat   Moist places, often in dense patches.

Range   Throughout North America.

146

Fairy Duster *Calliandra eriophylla*

This little shrub is an inconspicuous part of the arid landscape for most of the year, but in spring it makes its presence known with exquisite pink puffs of long stamens formed into feathery balls. The individual flowers are small except for their long stamens, and are showy only in the ball-like heads. Fairy Duster is a member of a large tropical segment of the pea family, which contains Acacias and Mimosas, mostly trees and shrubs which also have fluffy balls of flowers. The family relationship is evident in the narrow, small, pealike pods. Fairy Duster blooms from February to May.

Identification   A small, contorted shrub bearing puffs of pink flowers; leaves finely divided into tiny segments. Height: 8–20″. Flowers in dense heads nearly 2″ wide; petals reddish and tiny, inconspicuous beneath slender pink stamens ½–¾″ long. Leaves with 2–4 main divisions; each with 5–10 pairs of leaflets about 3/16″ long.

Habitat   Sandy washes and open slopes in deserts and arid grasslands.

Range   S. California to SW. New Mexico and NW. Mexico.

148

Tahoka Daisy *Machaeranthera tanacetifolia*

This is a close relative of the true asters (*Aster*), some of which have given rise to a popular, late-season garden plant called Michaelmas Daisy. Flowers in this genus, however, have very tiny spines, either at the tips of the teeth on the leaves or only at the tip of the leaf; plants of *Aster* do not. In western North America, there are perhaps 60 species in both genera; the very similar Sticky Aster (*M. bigelovii*) is a spectacular, vibrant purple wildflower of the southern Rockies, often seen along roads. The Tahoka Daisy blooms from May to September.

Identification   Flower heads with many narrow, bright purple rays; the bracts at the base of the head have tips bent or curled back; leaves fernlike. Height: 4–16″. Flower heads about 1¼–2½″ across, with a yellow, buttonlike center. Leaves 2–5″ long, divided into segments. Fruit seedlike, with short hairs lying flat on the surface and slender bristles on top.

Habitat   Sandy open ground in deserts or plains.

Range   Alberta to Texas, Arizona, and Mexico.

150

Salsify *Tragopogon porrifolius*

This immigrant from Europe, like the artichoke, lettuce, endive, and Jerusalem artichoke, is one of the few vegetables derived from the great sunflower family. Young spring leaves are edible, but the root is more popular; when cooked, it has a flavor like artichokes or oysters, and is given the name Oyster Plant. It often grows with its yellow-flowered kin, *T. pratensis* and *T. dubius*, and among them may occur rare, mixed-color hybrids that have given evidence for the origin of new species in the wild. Salsify blooms from June to September.

Identification   A purple flower head blooming at the swollen top of a sparsely leaved stem. Height: 20–48″. Flower head 2–3″ across; of small flowers, all with petal-like straps to one side. Leaves narrow, tapered; to 12″ long. Head matures into a lacy, tan globe, 4–5″ across; composed of many seedlike fruits, each with a feathery "parachute" on a stalk.

Habitat   Old fields, lots, and roadsides.

Range   Throughout North America.

152

Columbia Virgin's Bower *Clematis columbiana*

The Columbia Virgin's Bower, or Bell Rue, has woody clambering stems and pale bluish flowers with petal-like sepals but no petals. Later, feathery, silvery balls appear that make the plant as attractive in fruit as in flower. There are several other blue *Clematis* species within the range of Columbia Virgin's Bower, but they have more thoroughly dissected leaves. The sap of some species can cause blisters. This plant blooms from May to July.

Identification   A clambering or climbing vine; 1 bell-shaped pale purple to blue-violet flower appears on a leafless stalk, which grows from the angle formed by the leaf and the stem. Height: Climbing to 10'. Flowers with 4 lance-shaped, petal-like, purplish-blue sepals, 1¼–2½" long; many stamens at center. Leaves paired on the stem, each with 3 broadly lance-shaped leaflets, toothed or deeply lobed, each 1–2½" long. Fruit a silvery sphere, 2½" wide, composed of feathery plumes, each with a seedlike base.

Habitat   Woody or brushy areas in the mountains.

Range   British Columbia to NE. Oregon, east to Montana and Wyoming.

Blue Columbine *Aquilegia coerulea*

It is a wildflower hunter's delight to come upon the beautiful, nodding, blue-and-white flowers of Colorado's state flower. The Blue Columbine is a relative of the buttercup. Its petals have scooplike ends extending into nectar-filled spurs that reward the hungry hummingbird moth, which reciprocates by pollinating the flower. There are many species of columbine, in a variety of colors and sizes, and they have been hybridized to produce some of our most popular garden plants. Blue Columbine blooms from June through August.

Identification   Bushy plants with soft, divided leaves and blue-and-white flowers, tipped upward above the foliage. Height: To 3′. Flowers 2–3″ wide; petals modified into white scoops and spurs, petal-like blue sepals flared outward. Leaves soft, thin, divided repeatedly into fan-shaped leaflets ½–1¼″ long.

Habitat   Mountains; on moist slopes or aspen groves, or nestled in the protection of rocks.

Range   W. Montana to N. Arizona and N. New Mexico.

Baby Blue Eyes *Nemophila menziesii*

This charming wildflower often forms large patches, mingling with lupines and poppies, its delicate pastel-blue flowers contrasting with the bold colors of its neighbors. It has been cultivated in England for more than a century, and often is included in commercial wildflower seed assortments in the United States. The five petals are often paler near the base and are lightly speckled with tiny black dots. Its subtle beauty and easy recognition have made it a popular wildflower. It blooms from February to June.

Identification   Leaning, branched stems bearing near their ends delicate pale blue flowers with 5 petals; leaves divided into segments. Height: 4–12″. Flowers borne singly on slender stalks, 1–1½″ across; 5 petals with tiny black specks. Leaves ¾–2″ long; opposite one another on the stem, pinnately divided into segments, and with teeth along the edges.

Habitat   Grassy hillsides and flats, among brush, or in open woods.

Range   Central Oregon to S. California.

158

Redwood Sorrel *Oxalis oregana*

The Redwood Sorrel is one of the very few wildflowers common in dense redwood forests, where it forms an inviting carpet of cloverlike leaves. It is attractive in the woodland garden, but spreads fast on underground runners. In the same region, the rather similar Great Oxalis (*O. trillifolia*) is distinguished by having two or more flowers on a stalk. Other *Oxalis* species are yellow-flowered and particularly weedy. Bits of sorrel leaves add mild piquancy to salads, but it should be used moderately, for large amounts may be toxic. Redwood Sorrel blooms from April to September.

Identification	Low patches of leaves with 3 heart-shaped leaflets; 1 funnel-shaped, white or rose-pink flower on each stalk. Height: 2–7″. Flower ½–¾″ wide; with 5 petals, often with purple veins. Leaflets ½–1½″ long, often with a pale blotch in the center; heart-shaped, attached by points to the tip of erect stalk. Flower stalks and leaf stalks about the same length.
Habitat	Shady forests, including redwood groves.
Range	Coastal central California to W. and central Washington.

160

Western Starflower *Trientalis latifolia*

This trim little wildflower inhabits the sun-speckled floor of woods, its starlike, pale pink flowers held on slender threads above a neat ring of leaves. A count of several flowers will reveal that the number of petal lobes may differ from plant to plant, varying from five to nine. This species belongs to the primrose family, one of the few groups whose members have the stamens attached directly opposite centers of petal lobes rather than between them. A small swelling at the base of the stem gives this plant another common name, Indian Potato; but no modern reference indicates that it is edible. Western Starflower blooms from April to June.

Identification A delicate stem with a ring of 3–8 leaves at the top; 1 or more small, star-shaped pink flowers at the center. Height: 4–10″. Flowers about ½″ across, with 5–9 pointed petal lobes. Leaves broadly lance-shaped, 1¼–4″ long; all in a ring at the top of the stem.

Habitat Open woods and prairies.

Range British Columbia south through the northern two-thirds of California, east to N. Idaho.

Wild Blue Flax *Linum perenne*

The sky-blue flowers of wild flax readily drop their petals. The tough stems are full of fiber and difficult to pick; Native Americans made cordage from them. The stems of the related Common Flax (*L. usitatissimum*), a coarse annual with three-veined leaves, is the source of the linen fiber. To make linen, the stems must be retted (soaked in water until the soft tissue is rotted away); then the remaining fiber is treated to make it soft and pliant. Linseed oil is also pressed from the seed of this species. Wild Blue Flax, a perennial, blooms from March to September.

Identification   Slender stems with sky-blue flowers in loose clusters on fine stalks. Height: 6–32″. Flowers ¾–1½″ across; 5 petals, dropping readily. Leaves narrow, and pointed; ½–1¼″ long, usually oriented upward, almost parallel with stem.

Habitat   Well-drained soil in prairies, meadows, and open mountain slopes and ledges.

Range   Alaska to S. California, east to Saskatchewan, central Kansas, and W. Texas; also to N. Mexico.

Oregon Anemone *Anemone oregana*

In lowland woods in the late spring, low loose patches of stems appear, each bearing a single, starlike, pale blue flower. This is the Oregon Anemone. It is a member of the buttercup family, as indicated by its many stamens and ovaries. The Oregon Anemone lacks true petals; the pale blue flower is made up of sepals. It occasionally intergrades with the very similar white-flowered Western Wood Anemone (*A. lyallii*). The Oregon Anemone blooms in April and May.

Identification   Open patches of pale blue flowers with 5 petal-like parts on a single low stem. Height: 4–12″. Flowers 1½–2″ across; with many stamens. One leaf at the base, on a long stalk, divided into 3 lobes; 3 leaves in a ring just beneath the flower; each leaf divided into 3 main sections, each 3″ long; these sections sometimes further divided, making the leaves 5-lobed; lobes toothed or scalloped at tips. Fruit composed of many small, seedlike ovaries, nodding on the flower stalk.

Habitat   Moist open woods at low elevations.

Range   N. California to Washington.

Common Camas *Camassia quamash*

The six-pointed stars of Common Camas will often cover a meadow with a haze of blue-purple. It is one of the "Indian potatoes," a name applied to many of the bulbous plants that Native Americans used for food. Great care must be taken to distinguish this plant from the poisonous bulbs of the genus *Zygadenus* (the death camas)—another lily that grows in the same situation. Common Camas, one of two common species, is very slightly bilateral, the upper five petal-like segments sweeping slightly upward. Leichtlin's Camas (*C. leichtlinii*) occurs only west of the Cascades and the Sierra Nevada; it is nearer radial. Common Camas blooms from April to June.

Identification	Six-pointed, starlike flowers are light to deep blue-violet, held along a stalk above several narrow basal leaves. Height: 12–20″. Flowers 1½–2½″ wide, with 6 petal-like segments, 5 oriented up. Leaves to 2′ long, grasslike.
Habitat	Moist meadows.
Range	S. British Columbia to N. California, east to N. Utah, Wyoming, and Montana.

168

Elegant Brodiaea *Brodiaea elegans*

This member of the lily family is one of many in California that have purple flowers in tight or loose clusters atop a slender stalk. Although most brodiaeas are purple, a few are yellow or white, and one is red. They start to flower as the fields begin to dry at the onset of the hot weather. This species is distinguished from all others by the presence of white scales separate from, and shorter than, the three stamens. The very similar Ithuriel's Spear (*B. laxa*) is taller, has six stamens, and has a stalk beneath the ovary that is two or three times its length. Elegant Brodiaea blooms from April to July.

Identification Flowers purple, funnel-shaped, with 6 segments, held in a loose cluster atop a slender, leafless stem; leaves narrow, all at the base. Height: 4–16″. Flowers 1–1½″ long, with 6 petal-like segments; stamens 3, alternating with, and separated from, 3 flat scales that are shorter than stamens. Leaves 4–16″ long, and very narrow.

Habitat Grassy flats and hillsides.

Range N. Oregon to S. California.

Rocky Mountain Iris *Iris missouriensis*

This wildflower looks like the garden iris, its close kin.
The species is the only wild iris from the Rockies to the
crest of the Sierra Nevada and the Cascades. In the
terminology of horticulture, the declined petal-like sepals
form "falls," and the more erect petals are "standards."
The thick underground stems (rhizomes) of iris species
have been used by different cultures for fiber, to make
perfume and mask halitosis, and to treat disease. Rocky
Mountain Iris blooms from May to July.

Identification Large pale blue or blue-violet flowers atop a leafless
stem; leaves tough, fibrous, swordlike in outline. Height:
8–20″. Flowers 3–4″ wide; with 3 petal-like sepals
spreading out and down, and 3 erect petals toward the
center. Leaves narrow, flat; 8–20″ long.

Habitat Meadows and banks of streams, always where moisture
is abundant until flowering time.

Range British Columbia to S. California east of the Cascades
and Sierra Nevada (but isolated on the islands of Puget
Sound); east to S. New Mexico, Colorado, and North and
South Dakota.

Fringed Gentian *Gentiana detonsa*

The gentians are among the loveliest of mountain wildflowers, with large, deep blue or blue-violet, bell-shaped, fringed flowers. Several species of gentian are grown as ornamental or rock garden subjects. The many forms of the wide-ranging Fringed Gentian differ: The Rocky Mountain race has been called *G. thermalis* (for the hot springs in Yellowstone National Park, where it is the park flower); in the Sierra Nevada it is known as the Tufted Gentian (*G. holopetala*). Fringed Gentian blooms in July and August.

Identification	Stems often in a cluster, with several pairs of leaves and topped by bell-shaped, dark blue or blue-violet flowers. Height: 4–16″. Flowers 1¼–2″ long, with a bell-shaped base and 4 broad, flared, fringed lobes. Leaves lance-shaped, in 4–8 pairs on the stem; ½–2″ long.
Habitat	Meadows, bogs, and moist ground.
Range	Throughout most of the western mountains.

174

Cusick's Speedwell *Veronica cusickii*

This perky little plant is an unusual member of the snapdragon family. It has four blue or white petal lobes, the upper largest, and two stamens spreading to the side; this distinctive arrangement helps to identify other speedwells that grow in wet places, lawns, and gardens. Speedwells were used in teas to promote general health and to treat scurvy; this practice probably gave rise to the common name. Cusick's Speedwell blooms in July and August.

Identification Erect stems in little patches produce flat, deep blue-violet flowers with 2 stamens. Height: 2–8″. Flowers about ½″ wide, with 4 petal lobes, the upper broadest, the lower narrow. Leaves shiny, oval, bluntly pointed; ½–1″ long; borne opposite one another along the stem.

Habitat Open, moist areas in the mountains.

Range W. Washington to W. Montana, south to NE. Oregon and the Sierra Nevada of California.

Nuttall's Larkspur *Delphinium nuttallianum*

Larkspurs are lovely wildflowers, and several types have been developed as garden plants. But they are extremely poisonous to livestock; thus western ranchers seek to eradicate them from rangelands. In the Old West, gamblers administered one species, called Sleeproot, to throw off their opponents' game. The "lark's spur" of the name is the backward-projecting portion of the upper, petal-like sepal. Most larkspurs in the West are similar to Nuttall's, which blooms from March to July.

Identification Generally only one stem with a few roundish, divided leaves at the base. Flowers deep blue or blue-violet, bilateral, in an open cluster. Height: 4–16″. Flowers about 1″ wide, with 5 showy sepals and backward-pointing spur ½–1″ long. Petals 4; ³⁄₁₆″ long; blue or pale; lower ones deeply notched, the upper ones angling upward from flower center. Leaves round, to 3″ wide; divided into narrow, forked lobes.

Habitat Well-drained soil in sagebrush or open pine forest.

Range British Columbia to N. California, east to Colorado, Nebraska, Wyoming, and Montana.

Western Monkshood *Aconitum columbianum*

Western Monkshood is closely related to the larkspurs, and both are in the buttercup family. Like many of the larkspurs, this species is toxic, and it has been implicated in livestock poisoning. Early mountain shepherds called the hated plant Blueweed; it is also called Aconite, a modification of the genus name. The West has only this species, but another—Wolfbane (*A. napellus*)—is grown in gardens. Reputed to kill wolves, it figured importantly in werewolf lore of early times. The upper petal-like sepal resembles the hood of a monk's robe, giving the flower one of its common names. Western Monkshood blooms from June to August.

Identification   Tall, leafy plants with hoodlike, dark blue flowers in an open arrangement along the main stalk. Height: 1–7'. Flowers ¾–1½" high; 5 petal-like sepals, the upper one high arched and hoodlike, hiding 2 petals. Leaves roundish, palmately lobed and jaggedly toothed.

Habitat   Moist woods and mountain meadows.

Range   Alaska to the Sierra Nevada, east to the Rockies.

Miniature Lupine *Lupinus bicolor*

The windmill-like leaves and spires of pealike flowers ally this species with the giant garden lupine bred from another Pacific region species. The Miniature Lupine covers expanses of California fields with an amethystine hue, perfectly complementing the fiery orange of its companion, the California Poppy. Miniature Lupine blooms from March to May and, as in other species, the flower's pale spot turns pink in age as seed development begins, possibly signalling pollinating insects not to waste their time.

Identification An annual, often in patches; leaves windmill-like; flowers blue-violet and white, pealike, in rings on short, conelike spires. Height: 4–16″. Flowers about ⅜″ long; blue-violet; but upper petal has black-dotted, white central patch. The upper edges of the lower two petals (the keel) have a few hairs near the tip. Leaves palmately compound; segments ½–1¼″ long. Fruit a hairy pod about ¾″ long.

Habitat Open, often grassy places, from near sea level to middle elevations.

Range S. British Columbia to S. California.

182

Families and Their Members

Glossary

Alternate
Arranged singly along a stem, not in opposite pairs.

Anther
The tip of a stamen, containing pollen in 1 or more pollen sacs.

Basal
At the base of a stem.

Beard
A fringelike growth on a petal.

Bilateral
Having identical left and right sides.

Bract
A modified, often scalelike, leaf, usually at the base of a flower or fruit.

Calyx
Collectively, the sepals of a flower.

Clasping
Surrounding or partly surrounding the stem.

Cleft leaf
A leaf divided at least halfway to the midrib.

Compound leaf
A leaf made up of two or more leaflets.

Corymb
A flower cluster with a flat top, with the individual pedicels emerging from the stem at different points, blooming from the edges toward the center.

Cyme
A branching flower cluster blooming from the center toward the edges, with the tip of the axis always bearing a flower.

Duff
The partly decayed organic matter of the forest floor.

Involucre
A whorl or circle of bracts beneath a flower or flower cluster.

Leaflet
One of the leaflike parts of a compound leaf.

Lip petal
The lower petal of some irregular flowers.

Lobe
A segment of a cleft leaf or petal.

Node
The place on the stem where leaves or branches attach.

Opposite
Arranged in pairs along each side of a twig or shoot.

Ovary
The enlarged base of a pistil, containing the ovules, which will ripen into seeds.

Palmate
Arranged around a central point like fingers on a hand.

Pedicel
The stalk of an individual flower.

Pappus
A bristle, scale, or crown on seedlike fruits.

Pinnate
Arranged in two rows along an axis, like a feather.

Pistil
The female structure of a flower, consisting of stigma, style, and ovary.

Pollen
The grains containing the male germ cells.

Raceme
A long flower cluster with flowers blooming on small stalks from a common, central, larger stalk.

Sepal
One of the outermost series of flower parts, arranged in a ring outside the petals, usually green and leaflike.

Spadix
A dense spike of tiny flowers, usually enclosed in a spathe.

Spathe
A bract or pair of bracts, often large, enclosing the flowers.

Spike
An elongated cluster of stalkless flowers.

Spur
A tubular elongation of a petal or a sepal.

Stamen
A male structure of a flower, consisting of a filament and a pollen-bearing anther.

Stigma
The tip of a pistil, which receives the pollen.

Style
The stalklike column of a pistil.

Terminal
Borne at the tip of the main stem or shoot.

Tuber
A swollen, mostly underground stem with buds.

Umbel
A flower cluster with individual flower stalks growing from the same point, like the ribs of an umbrella.

Whorled
Arranged along a twig or shoot in groups of three or more at each node.

Index

National Audubon Society

THE NATIONAL AUDUBON SOCIETY is one of the largest, most effective environmental groups in the world. Headquartered in New York City, Audubon has over 500,000 members in 500 chapters, 9 regional and 5 state offices, a government-affairs center in Washington, D.C., and a network of more than 90 sanctuaries nationwide.

The National Audubon Society publishes *Audubon*, the award-winning conservation and nature magazine; *American Birds*, an ornithological journal; *Audubon Activist*, an environmental, grassroots newsletter; *Audubon Adventures*, a children's newsletter; and produces "World of Audubon" television specials.

Audubon's mission is to conserve wildlife and their habitats, to promote strategies for the wise use of our land, water, and energy sources, and to protect life from pollution, radiation, and toxic substances.

For more information, contact the National Audubon Society at 950 Third Avenue, New York, New York 10022. (212) 832-3200